# PIANO Praise & Worship

*Creative Piano Settings by FRED BOCK*

TABLE OF CONTENTS



Note: Those titles marked (*) are brand new arrangements and do not appear in any other Fred Bock piano collection.


I0809062

Fred Bock Music Company

# MAJESTY

Jack Hayford
*Arranged by Fred Bock*

**Strongly, with great intensity**

sub. p
mf

ff

f
f
rit.
fff a tempo
fff
fff
8ba

*for Roger Emerson*

# GLORIFY THY NAME

Donna Adkins
*Arranged by Fred Bock*

mp like a hymn
mf
p
mp
mf
f
mf
f
ff
8va (both hands)
mp

# THOU ART WORTHY

Pauline Michael Mills
*Arranged by Fred Bock*

Fine
(2x
8va
D.S. al Fine

*for Grant Matthews*

# SING HALLELUJAH TO THE LORD

Linda Stassen
*Arranged by Fred Bock*

slower
a tempo
f
slowing
a tempo
both hand 8va
mp
f
mf

# SEEK YE FIRST THE KINGDOM OF GOD

Karen Lafferty
*Arranged by Fred Bock*

stronger
mf
rit.

Meditatively
mp
mp sub.
f
ten. ten.
ten. ten.
l.h.
mf
p
both hands 8va
mp
pp

*for Joy MacKenzie*

# OUR GOD REIGNS

Leonard E. Smith, Jr.
*Arranged by Fred Bock*

**With warmth and movement**

mf
f
r.h.
f

ff
ff
ad lib.
l.h.
ff

*for Jan Sanborn*

# HE IS EXALTED

Twila Paris
*Arranged by Fred Bock*

**With exuberance and rhythmic drive**

1.
2.
mf
mf

f
ff
f
f
ff
8va (both hands)
8va

*for Gordon MacDonald*

# WE BRING THE SACRIFICE OF PRAISE

Kirk Dearman
*Arranged by Fred Bock*

**Bright and exuberant**

mf
l.h.
ff
legato
mf
ff
legato
mf
ff
l.h.
legato
mf

legato
ff
mf
mf
f
ff
r.h.
fff
8ba

# I LOVE YOU, LORD

Laurie Klein
*Arranged by Fred Bock*

**Prayerfully, and meditatively**

a little brighter
mf
ten.
mf
mf
mp
mf
mp
p
pp

# FATHER, I ADORE YOU

Terrye Coelho
*Arranged by Fred Bock*

ten.
ten.
mf
mp like the beginning
mp
mf
r.h.
mp
mp
l.h.
mf
slowly
mp
p
pp
ppp

# WE WILL GLORIFY

Twila Paris
*Arranged by Fred Bock*

strongly
f
r.h.
l.h.
ten.
mp
ten.
p
ten.
like the beginning
mf
mf
f
mf
mp
p

# O HOW HE LOVES YOU AND ME

Kurt Kaiser
*Arranged by Fred Bock*

ten.
l.h.
mp
ten.
a tempo
l.h.
r.h.
rit.
a tempo
f
rit.
mp
p
pp

# HIS NAME IS WONDERFUL

Audrey Mieir
*Arranged by Fred Bock*

stronger
mf
f
a little brighter
f
simile
r.h.
p subito
slowing
mp
mp
p
pp

# GIVE THANKS

Henry Smith
*Arranged by Fred Bock*

f
ff
l.h.

ff
mf
mp
mf
a little faster
ff

ten.
gradually slowing
ff
f
mf
mp
mp
slight accel.
rit.
pp

# HOW MAJESTIC IS YOUR NAME

Michael W. Smith
*Arranged by Fred Bock*

r.h.
l.h.

mp
broad and legato
subito
mp
mf
f
ff
8va
no ritard!
8va
fff
loco
loco